GRAPHIC LIBRARY™

UNIVERSAL MYTHS

DAWN OF TIME

CREATION MYTHS AROUND THE WORLD

BY NEL YOMTOV

ILLUSTRATED BY DANTE LIVIDINI

CAPSTONE PRESS
a capstone imprint

Graphic Library is published by Capstone Press,
1710 Roe Crest Drive, North Mankato, Minnesota 56003
www.mycapstone.com

Library of Congress Cataloging-in-Publication data is available on the Library of Congress website.
ISBN 978-1-5157-6629-2 (library binding)
ISBN 978-1-5157-6633-9 (paperback)
ISBN 978-1-5157-6637-7 (eBook PDF)

Summary: Find out how the world came to be according to seven creation myths from various mythologies
and traditions around the world — all told in gripping graphic novel format.

Editor
Abby Huff

Art Director
Nathan Gassman

Designer
Ted Williams

Media Researcher
Jo Miller

Production Specialist
Kathy McColley

Thanks to our consultant, Daniel Peretti, PhD, for lending his expertise and advice.

Design Element: Shutterstock: dalmingo (map),
ilolab, maradon 333, Milos Djapovic, NuConcept Dezine

TABLE OF CONTENTS

THE BEGINNING OF LIFE

Swirling black nothingness covers everything. There is no land, no sky, no plants, and no living things. Then suddenly, something emerges. A god breaks out of an egg. Serpents covered in bright feathers speak and life instantly appears on Earth. Can these things really happen? They can if you believe some of the world's most popular creation myths.

A myth is a story that explains a culture's connection to its past and its relationship with the world. A creation myth is a particular story that describes how life began. Creation myths may also try to explain the origin of the sun, the nature of good and evil, the mysteries of life, and much more. Nearly all cultures and religions — regardless of their age or geographical location — have some type of creation story.

Though each creation myth is unique, these stories often share common themes. In some myths, the universe starts with absolute nothingness. Or it begins with Chaos — the state in which everything exists in one swirling mass but has no individual shape. Soon, a great power or force starts to form things out of Chaos. In these myths, the creator makes the world by simply speaking, thinking, breathing, or even motioning. Creation from an egg or mud are also typical themes. Several different themes often appear in a single creation myth.

The following stories represent humankind's imagination and desire to make sense of life. They help answer one of the most basic questions that people have asked throughout time: *How did this world begin?*

CHAPTER ONE

RAVEN THE MAKER
AN INUIT MYTH

THE INUIT PEOPLE LIVE IN THE ARCTIC REGIONS OF CANADA, GREENLAND, AND ALASKA. THE INUIT HAVE SEVERAL DIFFERENT CREATION MYTHS, BUT THIS STORY ABOUT RAVEN IS ONE OF THE MOST TRADITIONAL. INUIT FOLKLORE OFTEN PORTRAYS RAVEN AS A TRICKSTER WHO PLAYS PRANKS ON HUMANS TO CAUSE MISCHIEF. HOWEVER, IN THIS MYTH, RAVEN IS A GOOD AND KIND CREATOR.

In the beginning, there were no people on Earth. The first man grew inside a pea pod and emerged fully grown.

I feel weak . . . I'm thirsty and hungry.

What's that? A bird-man?

I am Raven, and I made that vine. But I did not know anything like you would come from it!

Who are you? Where did you come from?

I came from the pea pod.

Hmm . . . you must be hungry. Wait for me here.

Raven changed back into a bird and disappeared into the sky.

Four days later, Raven returned . . .

I made these berries for you. Eat, and you will feel better.

In the days ahead, Raven formed clumps of clay into the shapes of sheep and reindeer.

By flapping his wings as a bird, the clay figures came to life.

As I made the other creatures, I also made you a companion. You will no longer be lonely.

7

Raven continued to create more animals to fill the earth. He explained the use of each creature to the man and woman.

The fish here will be good for food. Use the skin of the beavers for clothing.

All was good, but Raven grew troubled...

What if humans destroy everything I have created for their needs and pleasures?

I must make something they will fear.

You cannot kill all I have made. This bear will tear you to pieces if you disturb him. Hunt only what you need.

Soon three other men emerged from the pea pods. Raven taught the newcomers how to live.

He taught them how to make tools to hunt.

He showed them how to build canoes and log houses.

Raven made a wife for each man. In time, the couples had children.

Eventually, the earth became filled with people, animals, and living things of all kinds.

The people built a large village. They worked and played and lived in harmony.

DID YOU KNOW?

Ravens appear in many North American Indian creation myths. The bird is especially common in stories from the Pacific Northwest and Alaska. In some myths, Raven hurls a spear into the waters that cover Earth and brings up clumps of mud. He then uses the mud to create land. In others, he asks animals, such as ducks, to dive below the surface of the water in search of the special mud.

The world thrived, for humankind did everything that Raven had instructed them.

CHAPTER TWO
TEPEU AND GUCUMATZ
A MAYAN MYTH

THE ANCIENT K'ICHE' MAYA LIVED IN THE GUATEMALAN HIGHLANDS. THIS K'ICHE' MAYAN CREATION MYTH IS BASED ON A STORY IN THE *POPOL VUH*, AUTHORED IN THE 1500S. IN IT, SERPENT GODS BRING FORTH THE WORLD, BUT ALL DOES NOT GO AS PLANNED, AND THE TWO GODS STRUGGLE TO FIND THE PERFECT MATERIAL TO MAKE HUMANS.

At first, there was only the sky and the sea.

There was no land. There were no animals. There were no plants.

All was motionless and completely silent.

Only Tepeu [tay-PAYOO] the Maker and Gucumatz [goo-KOO-mats] the Feathered Serpent lived in the world. They were spirits with immense powers.

All is dark and empty, Gucumatz. It is not good.

Together we will bring light and life, Tepeu. Let us begin creating.

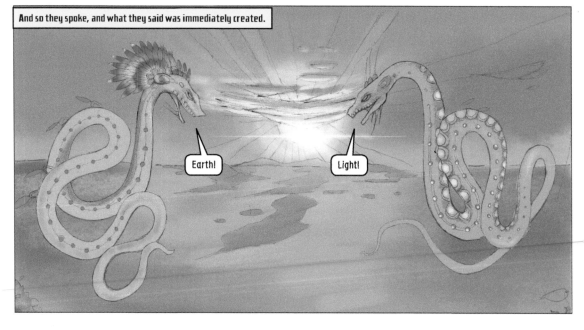

And so they spoke, and what they said was immediately created.

Earth!

Light!

Rivers! Forests!

Mountains!

As the spirits spoke, mountains and rivers came into being. Trees and plants of all kinds sprang up.

Tepeu and Gucumatz created animals to fill the earth and the skies. Each creature was given a voice. Birds sang, panthers growled, and snakes hissed. At last, the world was not silent.

But all was not perfect . . .

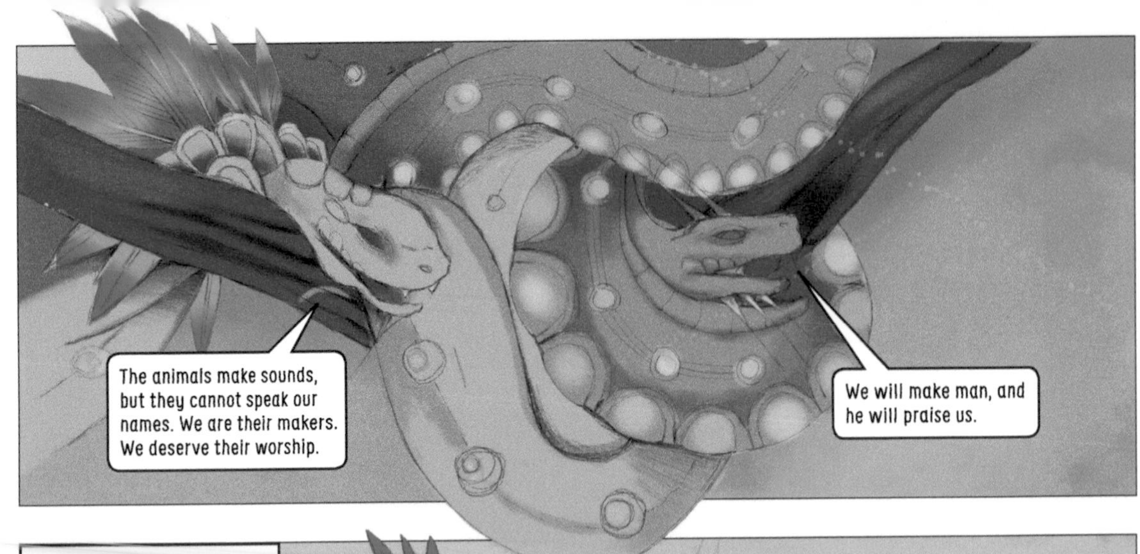
The animals make sounds, but they cannot speak our names. We are their makers. We deserve their worship.
We will make man, and he will praise us.

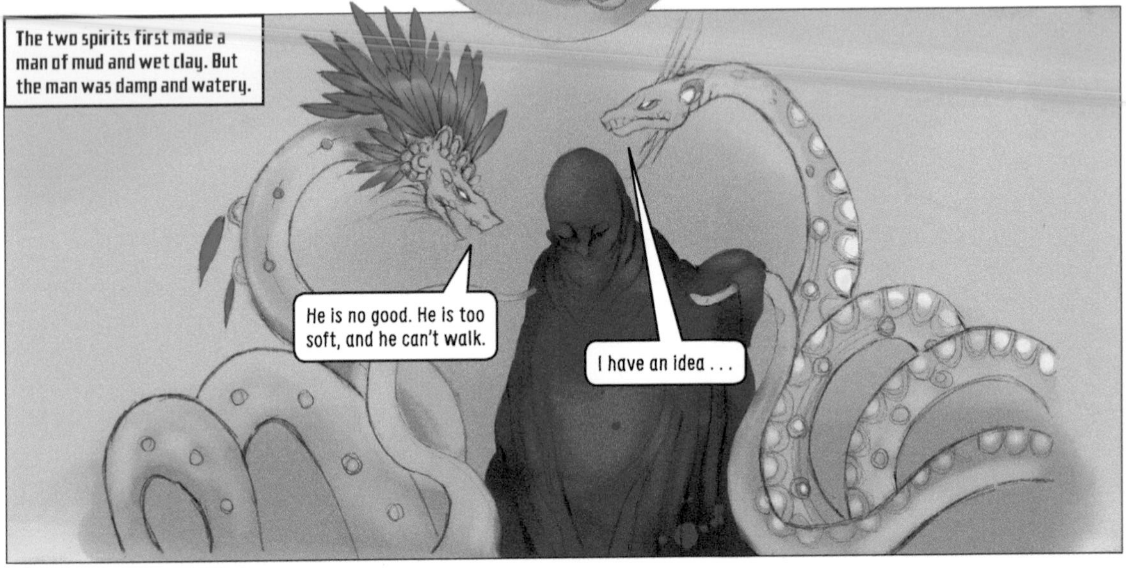
The two spirits first made a man of mud and wet clay. But the man was damp and watery.
He is no good. He is too soft, and he can't walk.
I have an idea . . .

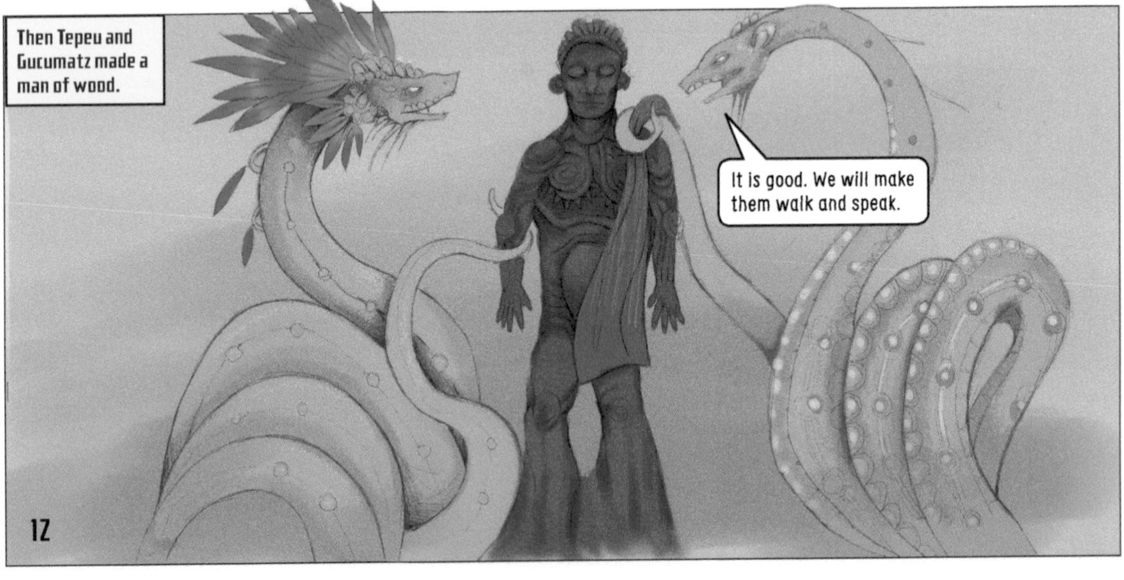
Then Tepeu and Gucumatz made a man of wood.
It is good. We will make them walk and speak.

The wooden people filled the earth, but they had no minds. They did not remember their creators. They did not praise them.

The creators were displeased.

These people are joyless and cold hearted! They do not laugh or smile. They do not love.

We must begin again.

Tepeu and Gucumatz decided to destroy the wooden people. They brought a terrible flood upon the villages.

Then large and small animals attacked the survivors. So did the wooden people's pots, plates, and other tools.

You treated us poorly. Now it is time for our revenge!

You were cruel and did not feed us.

It is said some of the wooden people fled to the forest to live in the trees. Today they are monkeys.

13

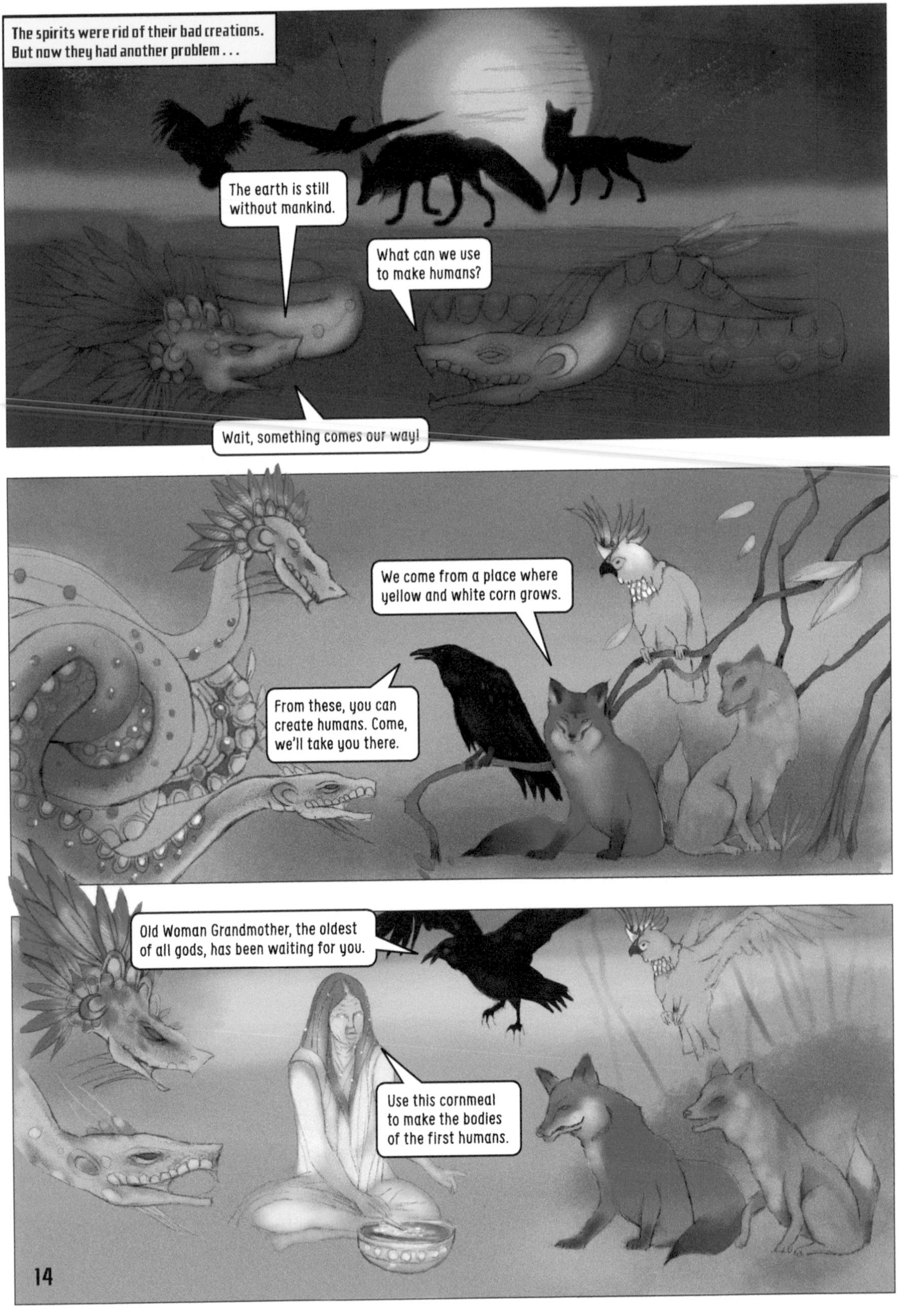
The spirits were rid of their bad creations.
But now they had another problem . . .
The earth is still without mankind.
What can we use to make humans?
Wait, something comes our way!
We come from a place where yellow and white corn grows.
From these, you can create humans. Come, we'll take you there.
Old Woman Grandmother, the oldest of all gods, has been waiting for you.
Use this cornmeal to make the bodies of the first humans.

The spirits took the cornmeal and created four humans. The men talked and walked. They were intelligent and had souls.

The four men also had great sight. They could see everything in the sky and everything on the earth. They instantly understood the world.

Praise to you for giving us sight and hearing! We have learned everything, great and small.

But the serpent spirits were worried.

They understand too much. They are almost too perfect.

You are right. We will remove some of their wisdom.

The spirits blew mist into the men's eyes. From then on, humans could only see what was nearby.

DID YOU KNOW?
The Feathered Serpent was a god found in many cultures in ancient Central America. Its Mayan name was Gucumatz. Among the Aztecs, who lived in the region from the early 1200s to 1521, the god was called Quetzalcoatl. The Aztecs made the Temple of the Feathered Serpent to honor Quetzalcoatl. Built about 1,800 years ago, the structure still stands in present-day central Mexico.

The humans no longer had complete knowledge of the world, but they were happy.

Tepeu and Gucumatz created wives for the men. Thus was the beginning of humankind.

15

CHAPTER THREE

RA, THE ALL-POWERFUL
AN EGYPTIAN MYTH

ACCORDING TO ANCIENT EGYPTIANS, BEFORE CREATION THERE WAS ONLY NUN — AN ENORMOUS BODY OF DARK, MOTIONLESS WATER. THERE WAS NO EARTH OR SKY. THERE WAS NO LIFE OR DEATH. IN SOME EGYPTIAN MYTHS, HOWEVER, FROM THIS VAST EMPTINESS CAME THE FIRST GOD — RA. WITH HIM CAME LIGHT, LIFE, AND ORDER.

In the beginning, everything was darkness. All that existed was Nun, the endless sea. Its great power gave rise to a mound of land. From the land came a large, shining egg.

In time, Ra, the all-powerful god, emerged from the egg. Ra was the first to be. He could take many forms and would be known by many names.

So great was Ra's power that whatever he spoke came into being.

I am Kheepara at the dawn and Atum in the evening.

At Ra's words, the rising sun, Kheepara, was created. Then the setting sun, Atum, also appeared.

Ra spoke the name Shu and the first winds blew. He uttered the name Tefnut and the first rains fell.

When Ra said the name Geb, the earth was created. He spoke the name Nut and the sky formed over the land. He named Hapi and the Nile River flowed.

With each element Ra created, a god of the same name also came into being. Shu, Tefnut, Geb, Nut, and Hapi were the earliest of the Egyptian gods.

Ra named everything on Earth. Each thing appeared and grew.

Yet the great god's work was not completed . . .

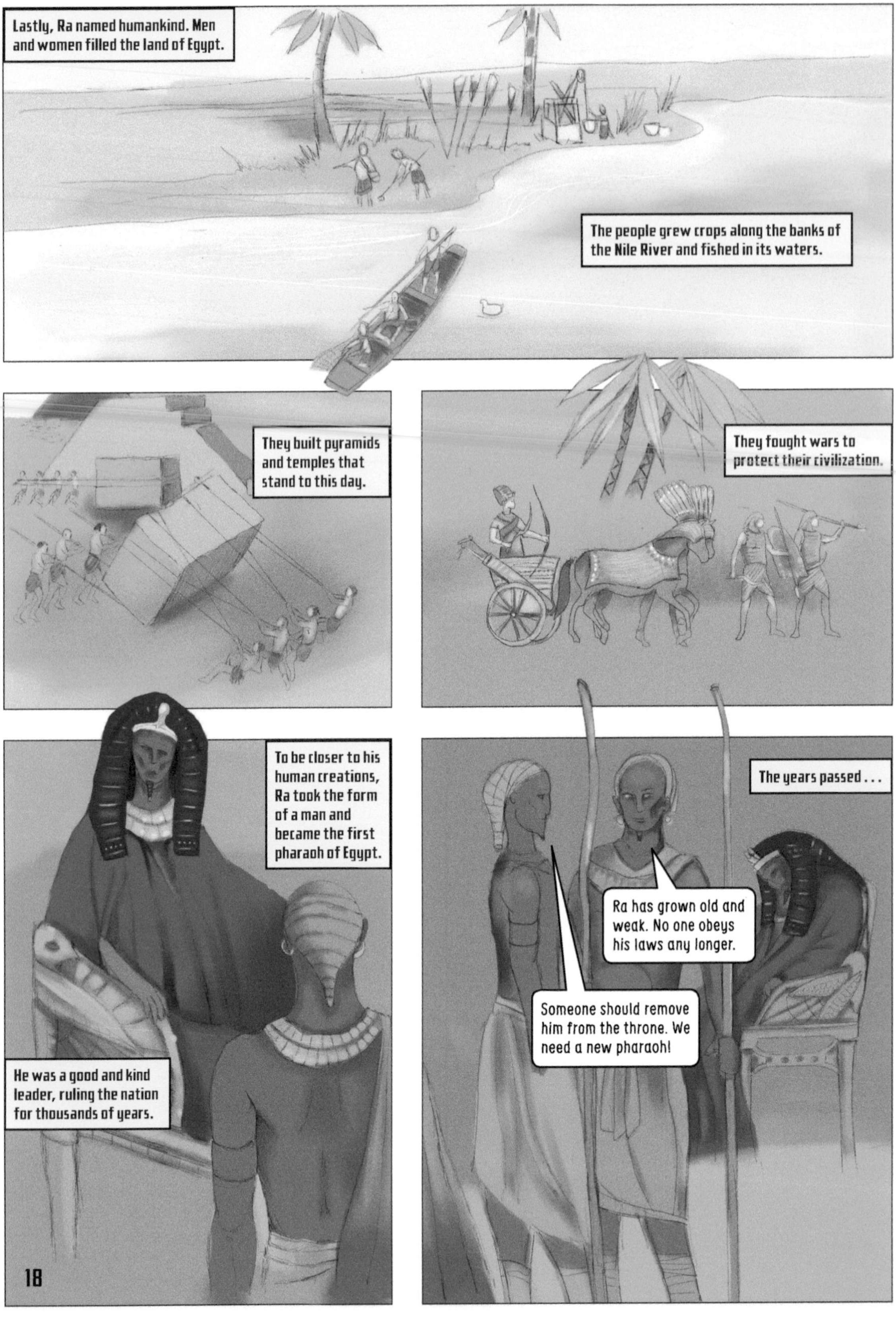
Lastly, Ra named humankind. Men and women filled the land of Egypt.
The people grew crops along the banks of the Nile River and fished in its waters.
They built pyramids and temples that stand to this day.
They fought wars to protect their civilization.
To be closer to his human creations, Ra took the form of a man and became the first pharaoh of Egypt.
He was a good and kind leader, ruling the nation for thousands of years.
The years passed . . .
Ra has grown old and weak. No one obeys his laws any longer.
Someone should remove him from the throne. We need a new pharaoh!

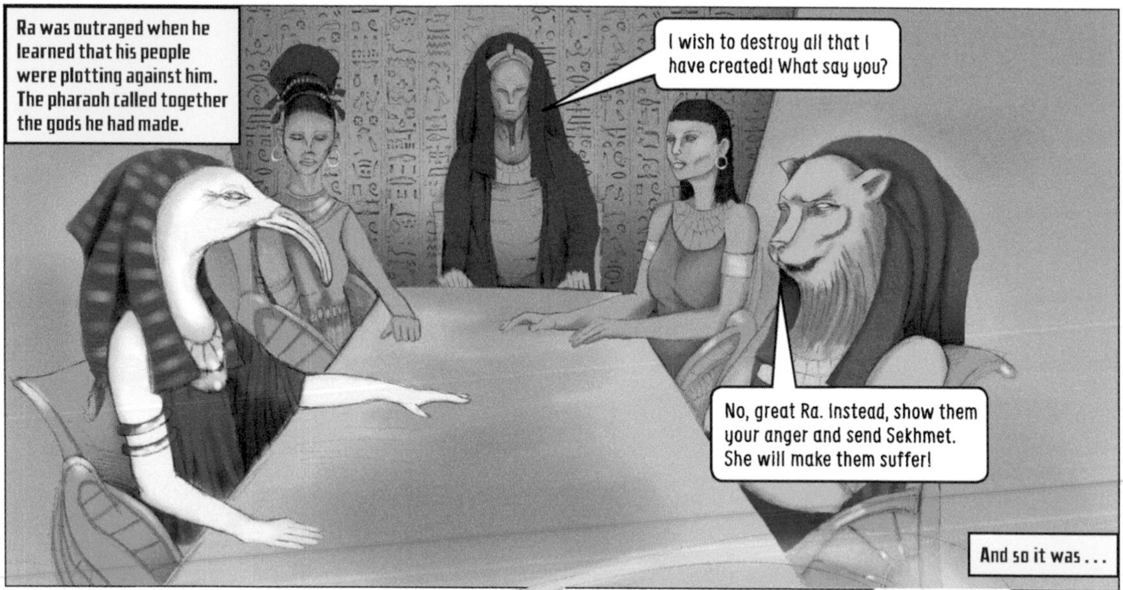

Ra was outraged when he learned that his people were plotting against him. The pharaoh called together the gods he had made.
I wish to destroy all that I have created! What say you?
No, great Ra. Instead, show them your anger and send Sekhmet. She will make them suffer!
And so it was . . .

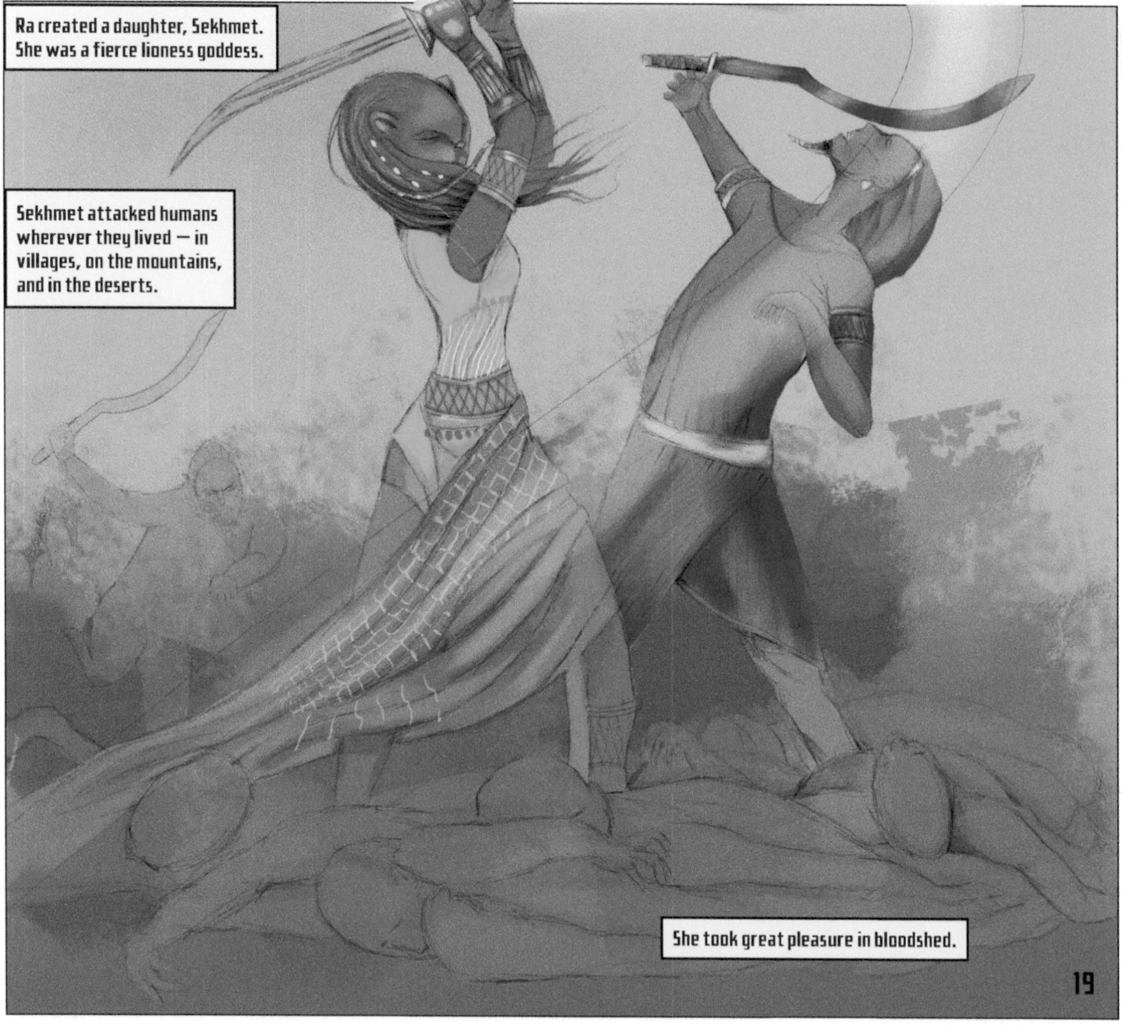

Ra created a daughter, Sekhmet. She was a fierce lioness goddess.
Sekhmet attacked humans wherever they lived — in villages, on the mountains, and in the deserts.
She took great pleasure in bloodshed.

Soon . . .

Have you obeyed my commands, Daughter?

Yes, Father, I bring death to humankind. My heart is happy.

Night after night, the lioness continued her rampage.

But soon Ra began to feel pity for his creations.

What have I done? I must find a way to stop Sekhmet from destroying my people.

Perhaps I can trick her . . .

Gather all the red ochre you can and bring it to the city of Heliopolis.

Did he say red ochre, the mineral that makes red dye? What could the pharaoh be planning?

Meanwhile, Ra commanded workers to prepare seven thousand jars of beer. He then told them to mix the red ochre into the liquid.

This looks like blood!

That night, men poured the beer onto a field where Sekhmet planned to kill the next day.

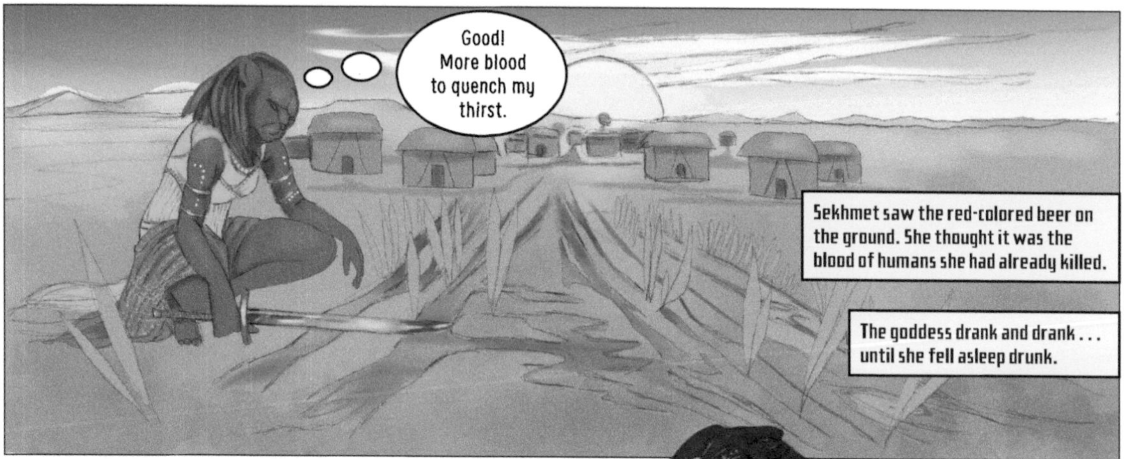
Good! More blood to quench my thirst.
Sekhmet saw the red-colored beer on the ground. She thought it was the blood of humans she had already killed.
The goddess drank and drank . . . until she fell asleep drunk.

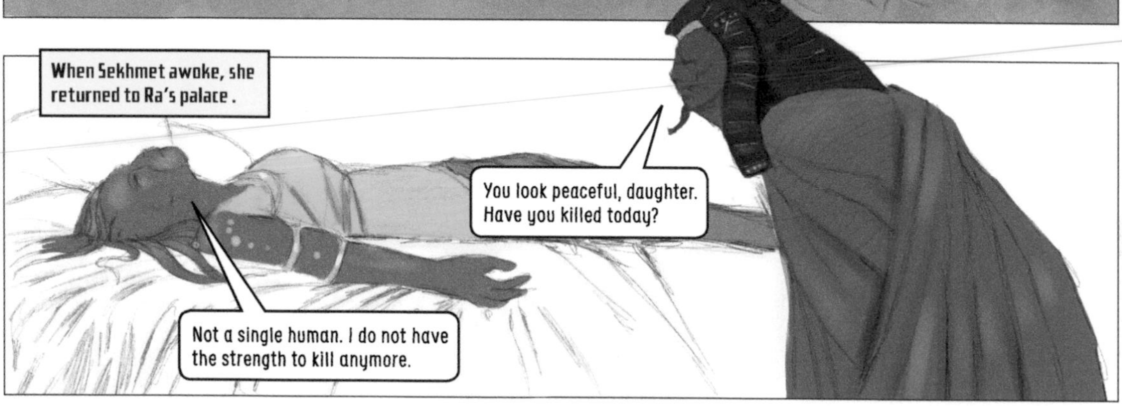
When Sekhmet awoke, she returned to Ra's palace .
You look peaceful, daughter. Have you killed today?
Not a single human. I do not have the strength to kill anymore.

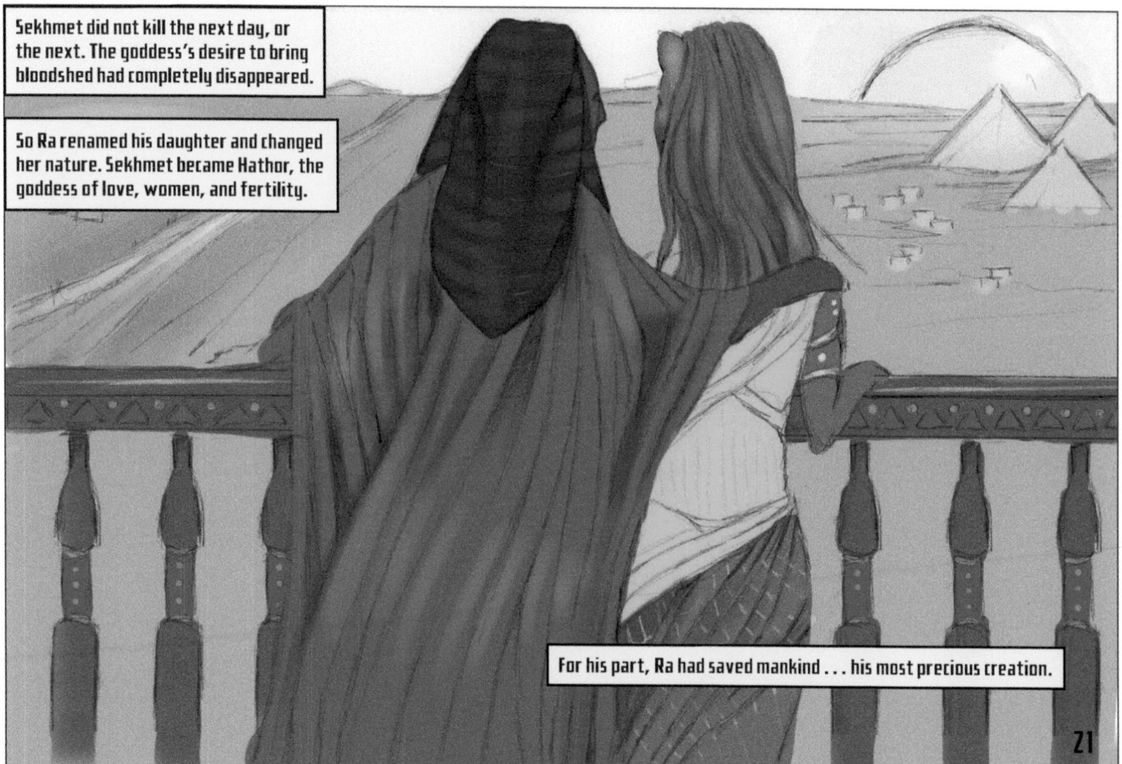
Sekhmet did not kill the next day, or the next. The goddess's desire to bring bloodshed had completely disappeared.
So Ra renamed his daughter and changed her nature. Sekhmet became Hathor, the goddess of love, women, and fertility.
For his part, Ra had saved mankind . . . his most precious creation.

CHAPTER FOUR

NYAMBE, THE CREATOR

A LOZI MYTH

IN THIS MYTH OF THE LOZI PEOPLE OF ZAMBIA, THE CREATOR FLEES FROM THE VERY PEOPLE HE MADE. NYAMBE, THE CREATOR, IS UPSET BY THE AGGRESSIVE WAYS OF HUMANS AND HOW THEY IMITATE HIM. SO NYAMBE CLIMBS UP TO THE HEAVENS TO LIVE IN PEACE. ONCE THERE, THE SUN BECOMES HIS SYMBOL TO HUMANS.

Ages ago, the god Nyambe and his wife, Nasilele, lived on Earth. Through his thoughts, the powerful god created all that existed.

He made the mountains, rivers, forests, and valleys. He created the animals on the land, the birds in the skies, and the fish in the oceans.

Nyambe also created the first people, Kamunu and his wife.

Everything I do, Kamunu does. When I carve a bowl, he carves his own bowl. When I forge metals, he does the same.

He is too intelligent. I'm beginning to fear this creation of mine.

One day, Kamunu made an iron spear. He used it to kill an antelope, which he ate. Nyambe was enraged.

Why do you kill? You are all brothers . . . you are all my children! Leave here, and do not return!

But one year later . . .

Please, Nyambe. Give me land to farm, so I won't have to kill the animals.

So shall it be.

One night, a deer ran onto Kamunu's fields and started to trample his crops. So he killed the animal.

But Nyambe was not upset this time. Instead, he allowed Kamunu to eat the deer as a present.

The next day . . .

My dog has died.

That is the way of the world.

23

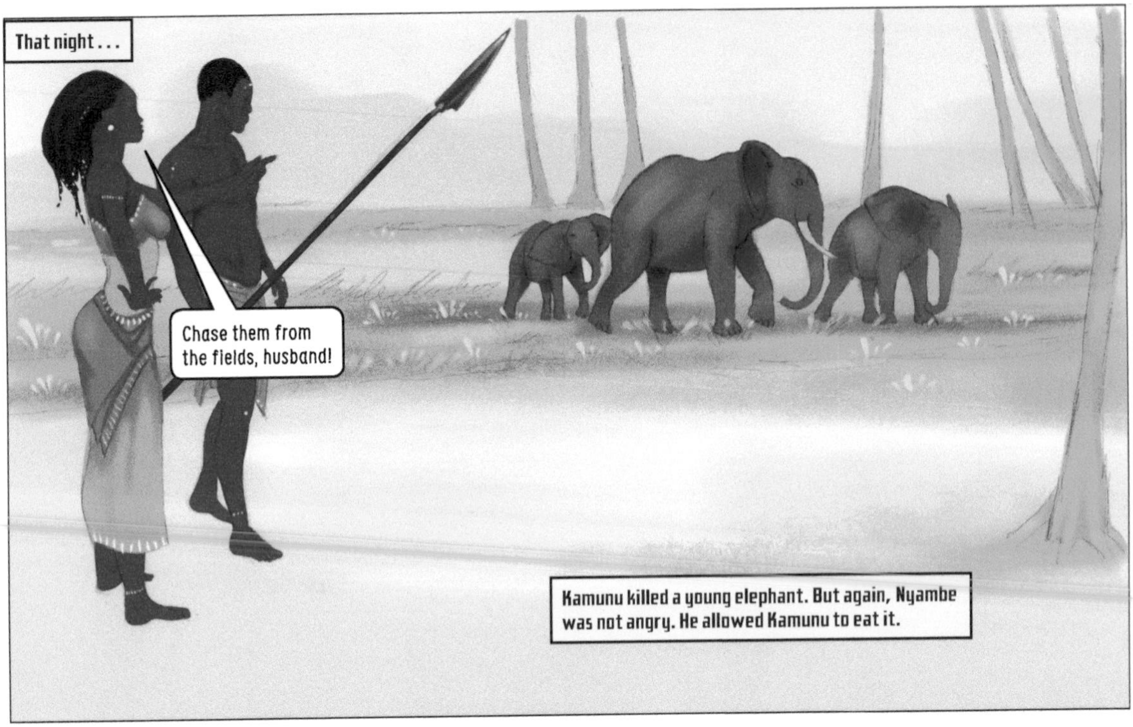
That night . . .
Chase them from the fields, husband!
Kamunu killed a young elephant. But again, Nyambe was not angry. He allowed Kamunu to eat it.

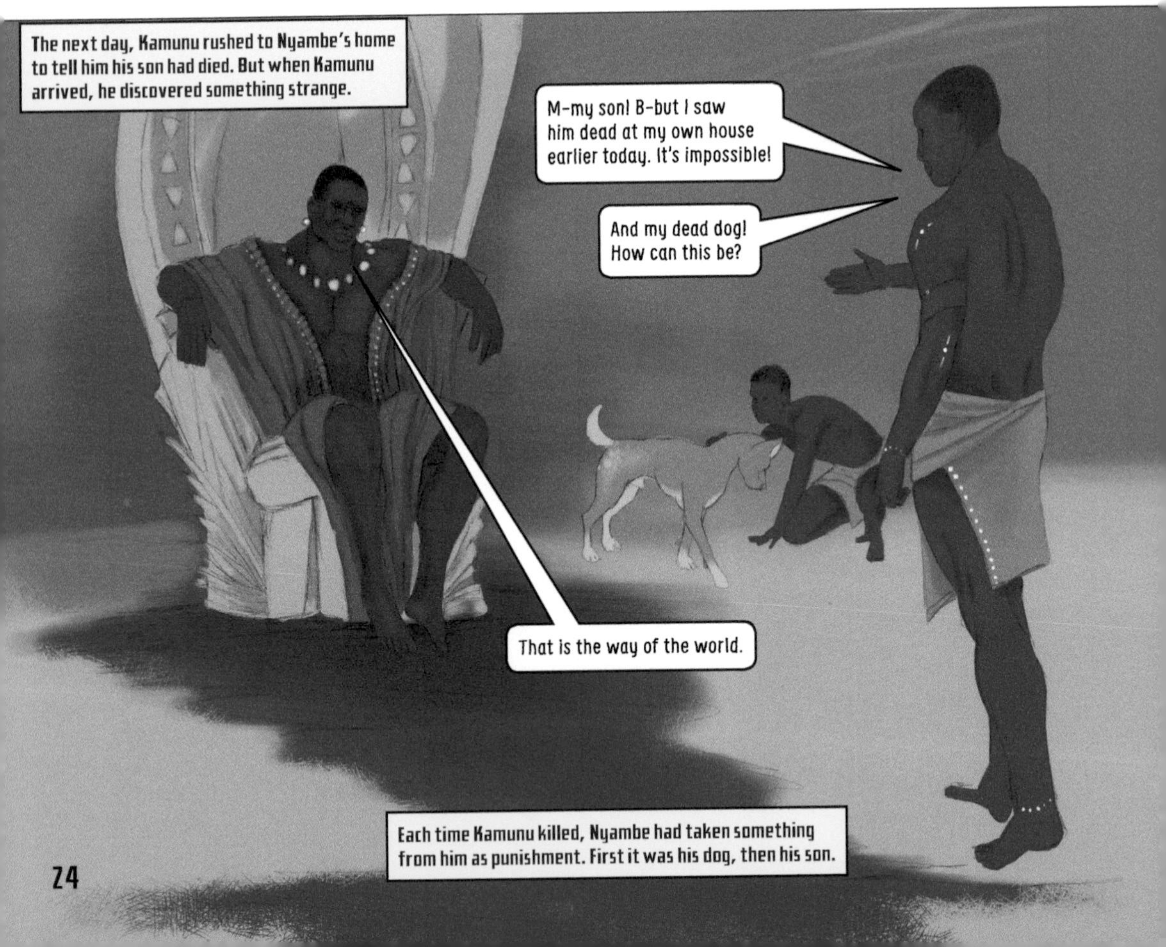
The next day, Kamunu rushed to Nyambe's home to tell him his son had died. But when Kamunu arrived, he discovered something strange.
M-my son! B-but I saw him dead at my own house earlier today. It's impossible!
And my dead dog! How can this be?
That is the way of the world.
Each time Kamunu killed, Nyambe had taken something from him as punishment. First it was his dog, then his son.

Later, Nyambe called a council of his favorite creatures, Kangomba the antelope and Sasisho, a messenger bird.

Kamunu bothers us constantly, and he will destroy everything. We must leave this place if we are to live in peace.

Let us go to an island. There we will be free of Kamunu.

But Kamunu wanted to be near his creator. He built a raft and sailed to Nyambe's new home.

Nyambe! Nyambe!

He has found us! What bad luck.

Nyambe raised a mountain from the earth and went to live there.

But again, Kamunu found his maker.

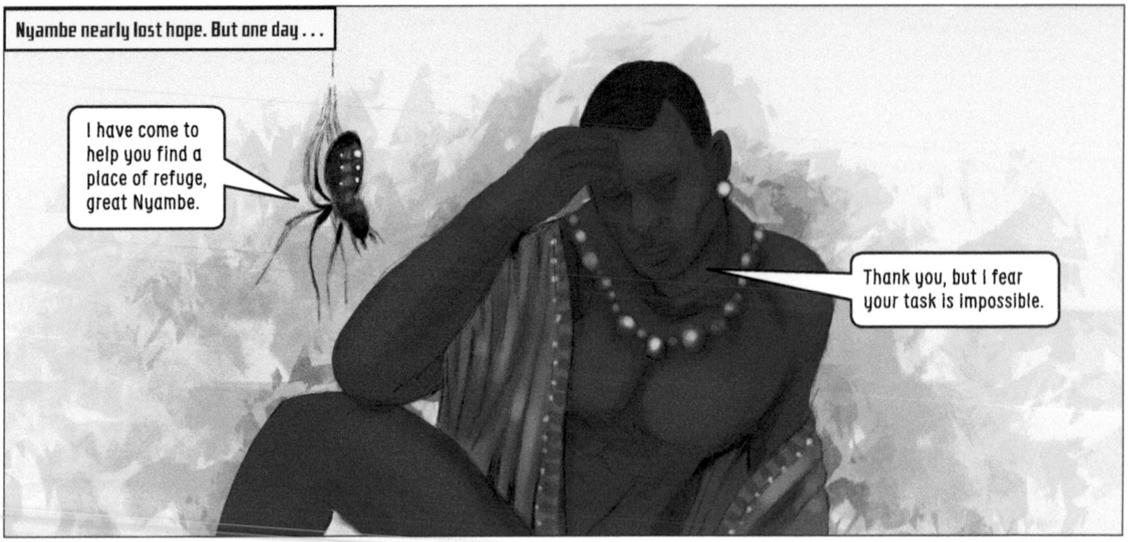
Nyambe nearly lost hope. But one day . . .
I have come to help you find a place of refuge, great Nyambe.
Thank you, but I fear your task is impossible.

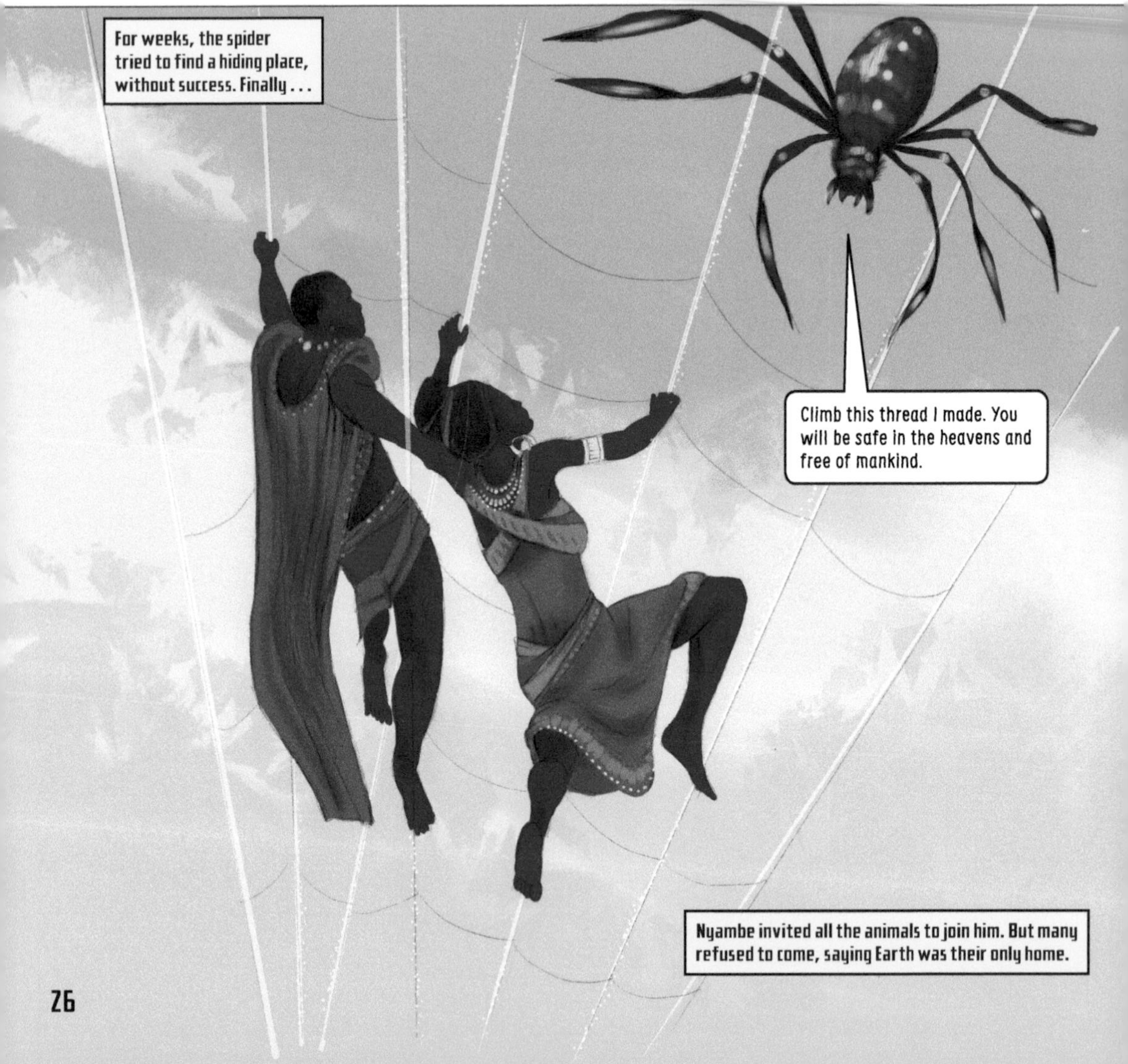
For weeks, the spider tried to find a hiding place, without success. Finally . . .
Climb this thread I made. You will be safe in the heavens and free of mankind.
Nyambe invited all the animals to join him. But many refused to come, saying Earth was their only home.

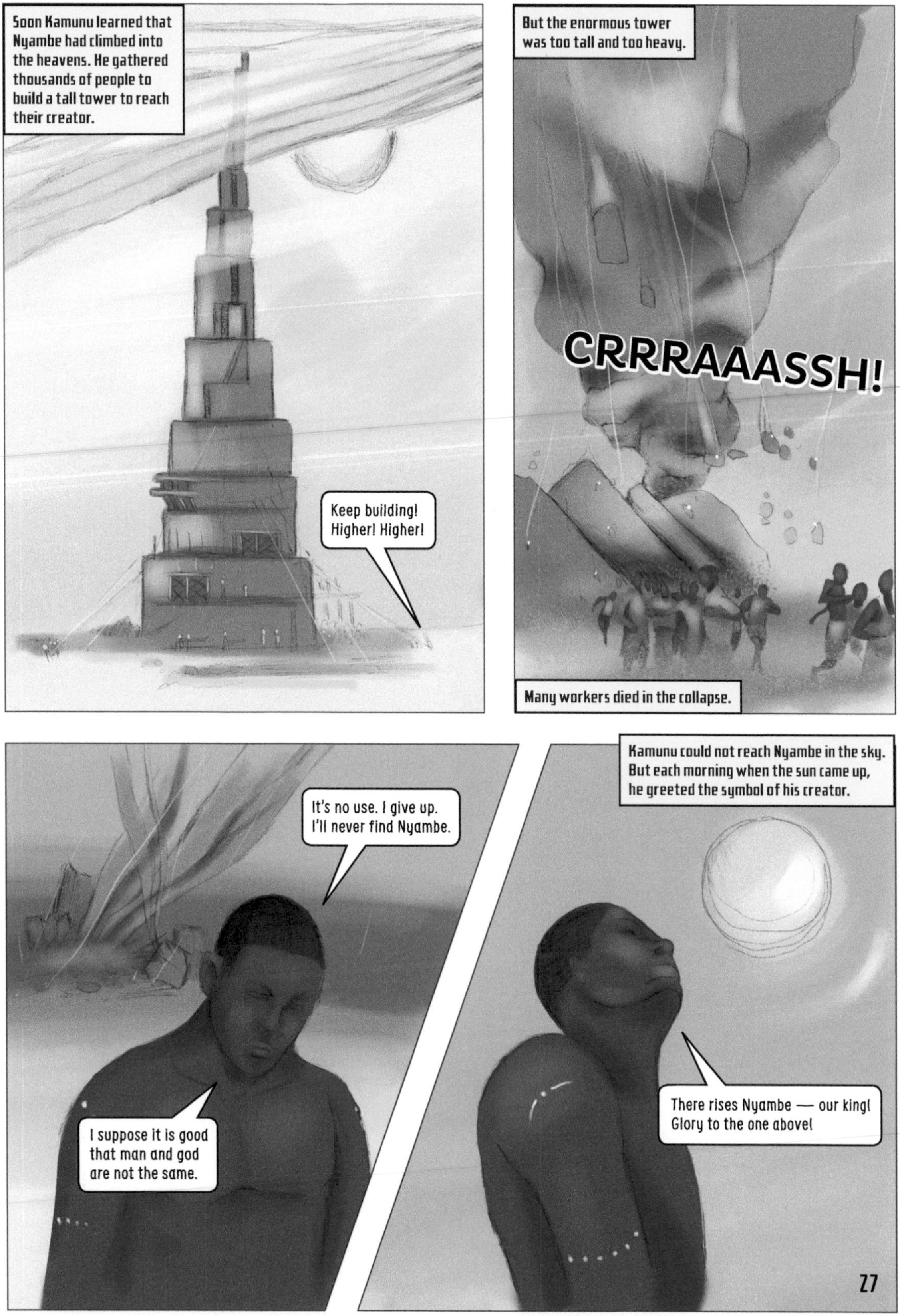
Soon Kamunu learned that Nyambe had climbed into the heavens. He gathered thousands of people to build a tall tower to reach their creator.
Keep building! Higher! Higher!
But the enormous tower was too tall and too heavy.
CRRRAAASSH!
Many workers died in the collapse.
It's no use. I give up. I'll never find Nyambe.
I suppose it is good that man and god are not the same.
Kamunu could not reach Nyambe in the sky. But each morning when the sun came up, he greeted the symbol of his creator.
There rises Nyambe — our king! Glory to the one above!

CHAPTER FIVE
YMIR, THE FROST GIANT
A NORSE MYTH

FOR CENTURIES, THE NORSE TOLD STORIES THAT EXPLAINED CREATION. IN THE EARLY 13TH CENTURY, MANY OF THE MYTHS WERE WRITTEN DOWN IN A BOOK CALLED THE *PROSE EDDA*. THE FOLLOWING TALE FROM THE *PROSE EDDA* TELLS OF HOW THREE BROTHER GODS CRAFTED THE COSMOS FROM THE REMAINS OF AN EVIL GIANT'S BODY.

In the beginning, there were two regions. Niflheim was in the north and was full of ice. Muspelheim lay in the south and burned hot with fire.

Between them was Ginnungagap [GIN-oong-gah-GAHP], a large space full of nothing but mist. When the ice and fire from the other regions met in Ginnungagap, water formed.

From the water came a frost giant called Ymir [EE-mir]. The giant was the first being, but he was evil. With each drop of sweat that fell from Ymir, a new frost giant was born.

Then something else formed in the melting ice of Ginnungagap. It was giant cow. The cow licked a block of ice until a person emerged. His name was Buri, the first god.

Buri married the daughter of a frost giant. Eventually, they had three grandsons — the gods Odin, Vili, and Ve. The brother gods hated Ymir.

Ymir and the pack of giants he has fathered are horrible creatures.

Something must be done.

Odin, Vili, and Ve killed Ymir. They carried him to Ginnungagap. Then the brothers began to create the world from the giant's body.

The three gods made the earth from Ymir's flesh and the mountains from his bones.

They formed the sky from the giant's skull.

Boulders and stones were made from Ymir's teeth and jaws. His blood became the lakes and the seas.

The brothers gathered sparks and glowing embers from Muspelheim. From these, they made the sun, moon, and stars.

The brothers also created nine worlds from Ymir's body. Yggdrasill, a giant ash tree, nourished the worlds with its roots. Known as the World Tree, Yggdrasill gave life to all that existed in the Norse universe.

The brothers built Asgard, a place of magnificent palaces. It was linked to Midgard, the world of humans, by a rainbow bridge called Bifrost.

Asgard shall be home for us and the Aesir gods to come.

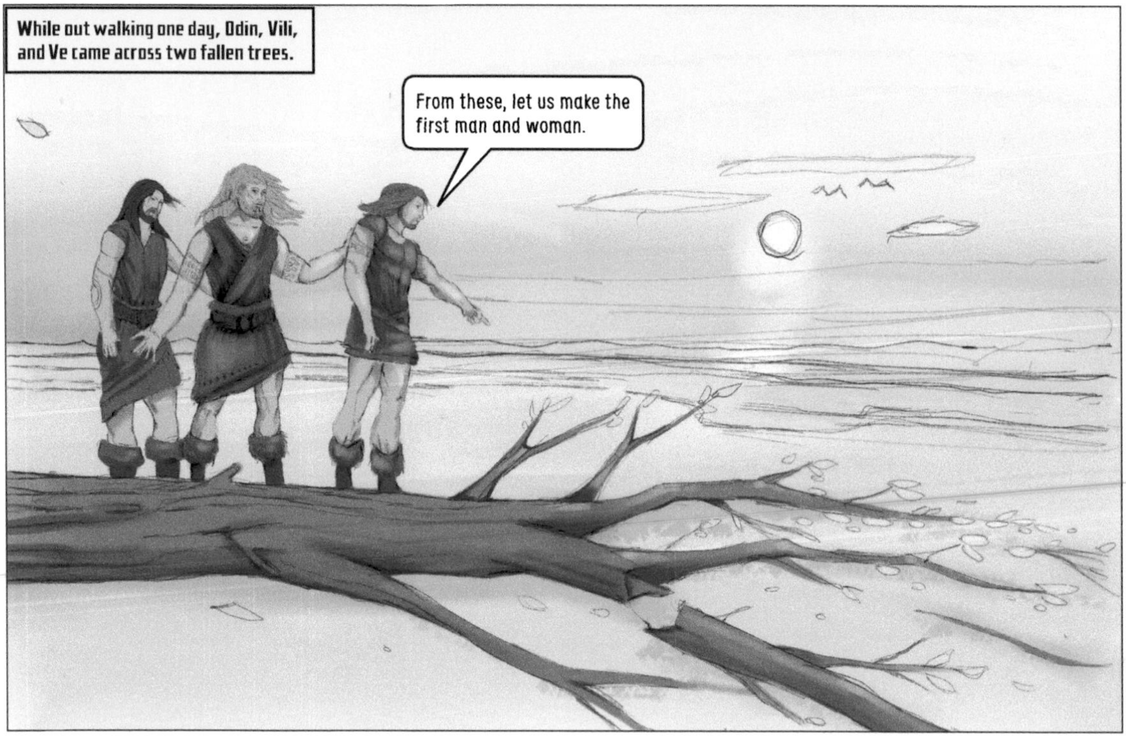
While out walking one day, Odin, Vili, and Ve came across two fallen trees.
From these, let us make the first man and woman.

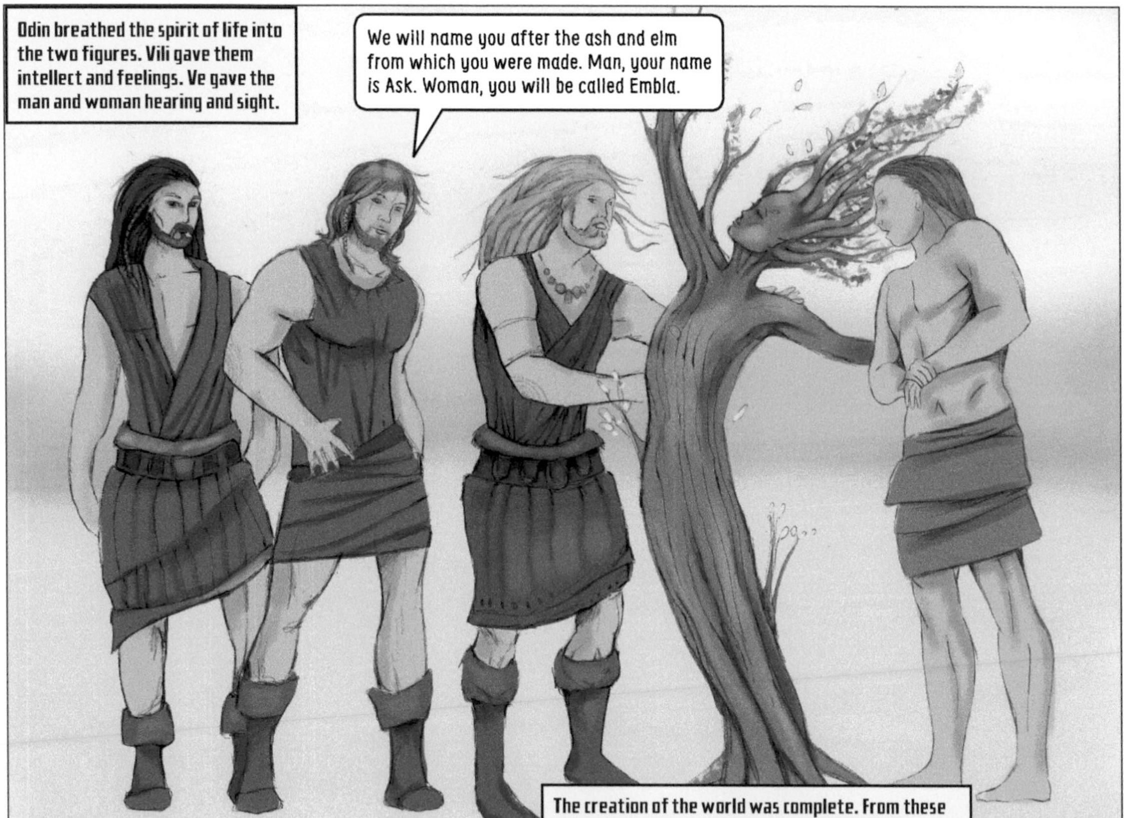
Odin breathed the spirit of life into the two figures. Vili gave them intellect and feelings. Ve gave the man and woman hearing and sight.
We will name you after the ash and elm from which you were made. Man, your name is Ask. Woman, you will be called Embla.
The creation of the world was complete. From these first people were born the races of humankind. And it all came to be from the body of Ymir, the frost giant.

CHAPTER SIX

PAN GU, BORN FROM THE COSMIC EGG

A CHINESE MYTH

THE CHINESE PRE-CREATION UNIVERSE WAS IN THE FORM OF AN EGG. IN FACT, THE CHINESE CULTURE HAS SEVERAL VERSIONS OF THE CREATION-FROM-EGG MYTH. THE FOLLOWING STORY SHOWS THREE OF THE MOST WELL KNOWN ACCOUNTS. EACH TALE FEATURES A STRANGE-LOOKING, BUT KINDLY, GOD CALLED PAN GU.

In the beginning, there was only the great egg. Inside was Chaos, a swirling mass of opposites. Cold and heat, dark and light, male and female all existed together.

For 18,000 years, the egg remained unchanged.

One day, the egg began to crack. A force from inside pushed the eggshell open.

Pan Gu, the first being, burst from the egg. The great creator of all to come was finally born.

CRRRAACK!

33

He pushed the top half of the eggshell upward until it became the sky above. The bottom half of the eggshell formed the earth beneath.

For 18,000 years, Pan Gu grew 10 feet each day, pushing the sky and earth farther apart. Horns grew from his head and large tusks grew from his upper jaw.

When he had finished growing, Pan Gu carved out deep valleys and made paths for mighty rivers.

He piled up earth to create towering mountains.

Pan Gu created the vast seas and placed them where they remain to this day.

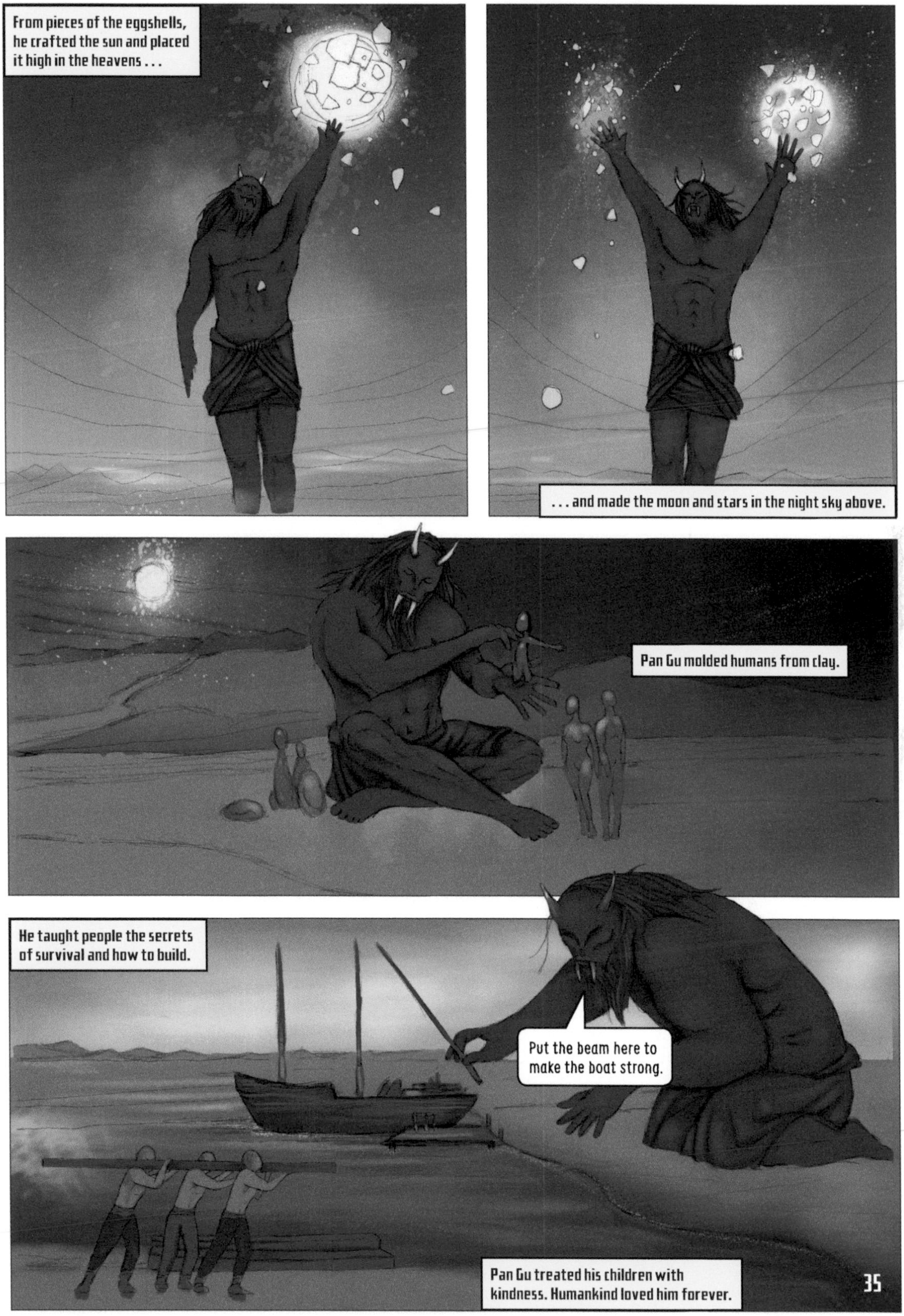
From pieces of the eggshells, he crafted the sun and placed it high in the heavens . . .
. . . and made the moon and stars in the night sky above.
Pan Gu molded humans from clay.
He taught people the secrets of survival and how to build.
Put the beam here to make the boat strong.
Pan Gu treated his children with kindness. Humankind loved him forever.

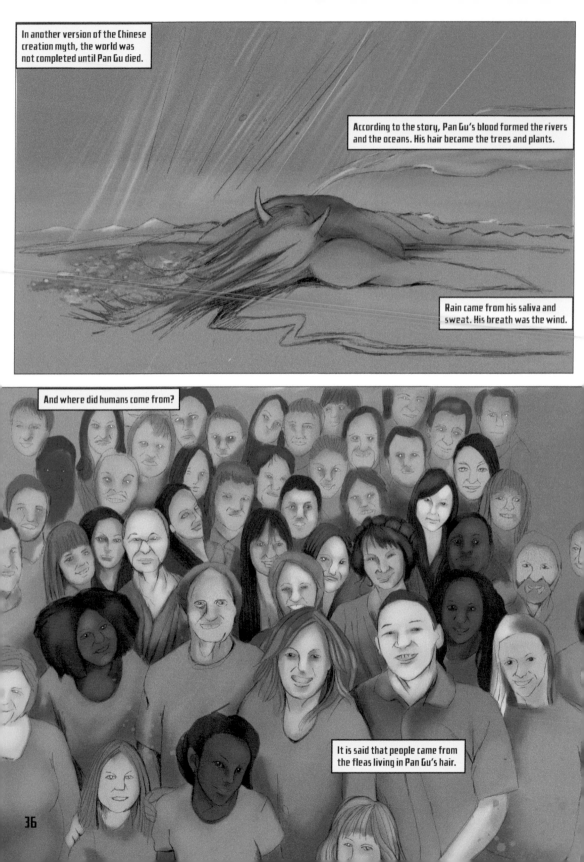

In another version of the Chinese creation myth, the world was not completed until Pan Gu died.

According to the story, Pan Gu's blood formed the rivers and the oceans. His hair became the trees and plants.

Rain came from his saliva and sweat. His breath was the wind.

And where did humans come from?

It is said that people came from the fleas living in Pan Gu's hair.

In some regions of China, people tell a third story of the creation.

When Pan Gu cried, his tears became the mighty Yellow River.

And when he died, his body formed the Sacred Mountains of China. One mountain rose from his head, and another from his body. Other mountains came from his arms and his feet.

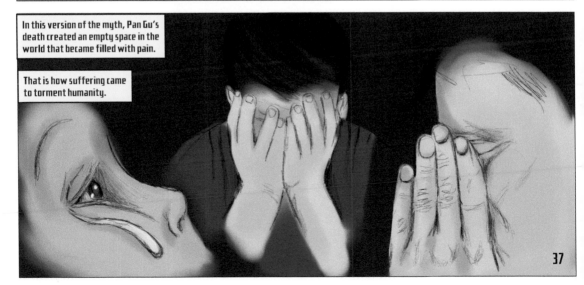

In this version of the myth, Pan Gu's death created an empty space in the world that became filled with pain.

That is how suffering came to torment humanity.

37

CHAPTER SEVEN

ILMATAR, THE GODDESS OF AIR

A FINNO-UGRIC MYTH

THE FINNO-UGRIC PEOPLES LIVE IN EUROPE, FROM AN AREA THAT STRETCHES FROM NORWAY TO SIBERIA AND DOWN TO THE DANUBE RIVER. THIS STORY APPEARS IN THE *KALEVALA*, A BOOK PUBLISHED IN 1849 THAT CONTAINS FINNISH MYTHS AND FOLKLORE. IN THIS MYTH, THE GODDESS ILMATAR (**IHL**-MAH-TAHR) WANTS TO CREATE LIFE. WITH THE HELP OF A BEAUTIFUL BIRD, SHE FINALLY REALIZES HER DREAM.

In the beginning, only Sky and dark waters existed. Sky's daughter was Ilmatar.

One day, while wandering the empty, endless Sky, Ilmatar floated down to rest upon the waters.

For 700 years, Ilmatar floated in the vast ocean, tossed to and fro by powerful waves and winds. She wished she had not left Sky, and soon she became lonely.

Sigh. I'm tired of being thrown around by the water. I wish there was more life here, but how can I create it?

Then one day, Ilmatar found the gods had listened to her. A duck appeared, flying through the air. Ilmatar was no longer alone.

Such a beautiful creature! I've never seen anything like it before. It must be looking for a place to land.

I must be still, so it does not fly away.

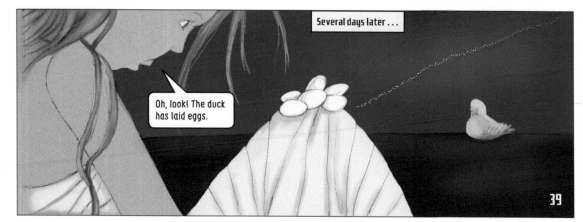

Several days later . . .

Oh, look! The duck has laid eggs.

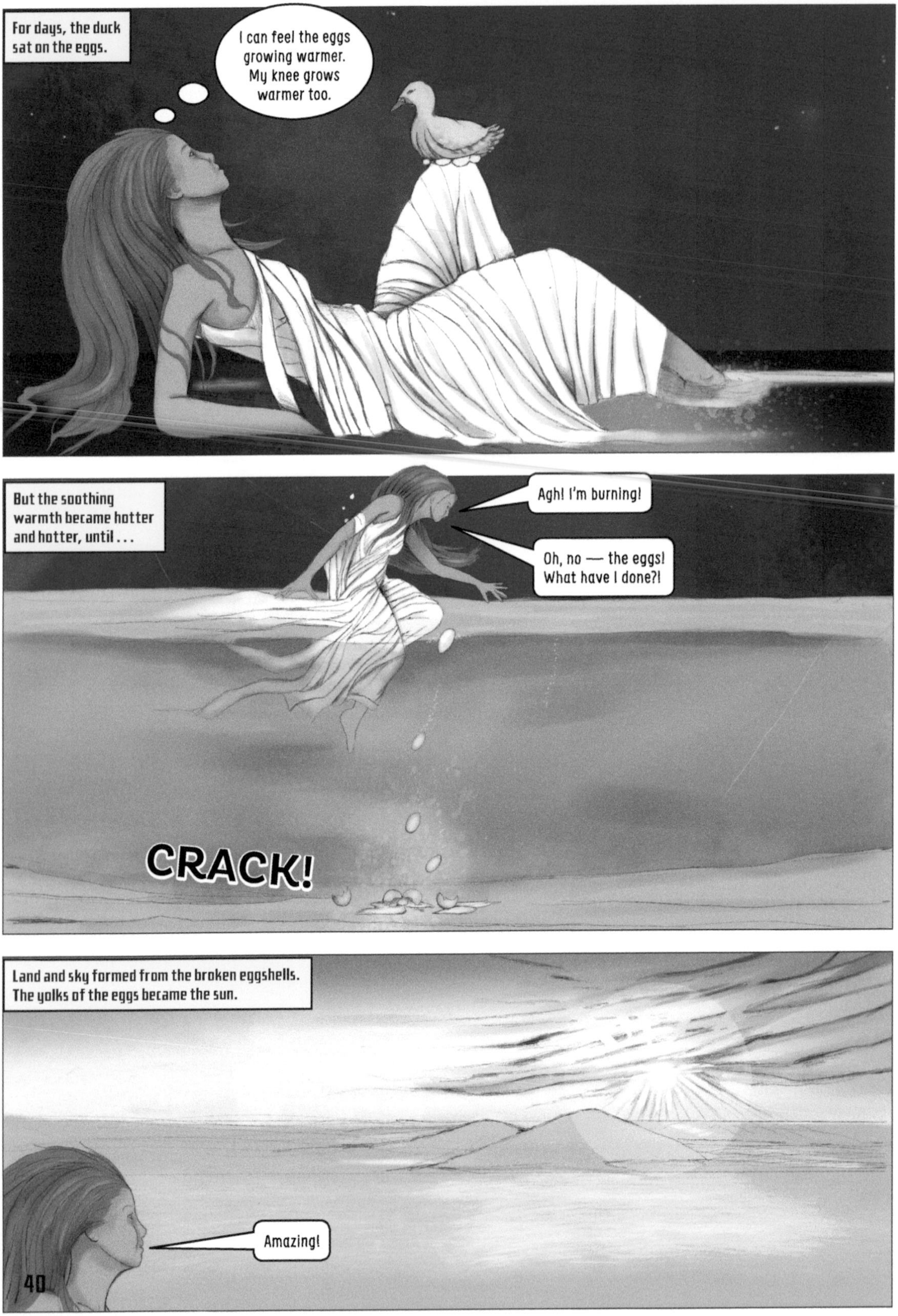
For days, the duck sat on the eggs.
I can feel the eggs growing warmer. My knee grows warmer too.
But the soothing warmth became hotter and hotter, until . . .
Agh! I'm burning!
Oh, no — the eggs! What have I done?!
CRACK!
Land and sky formed from the broken eggshells. The yolks of the eggs became the sun.
Amazing!

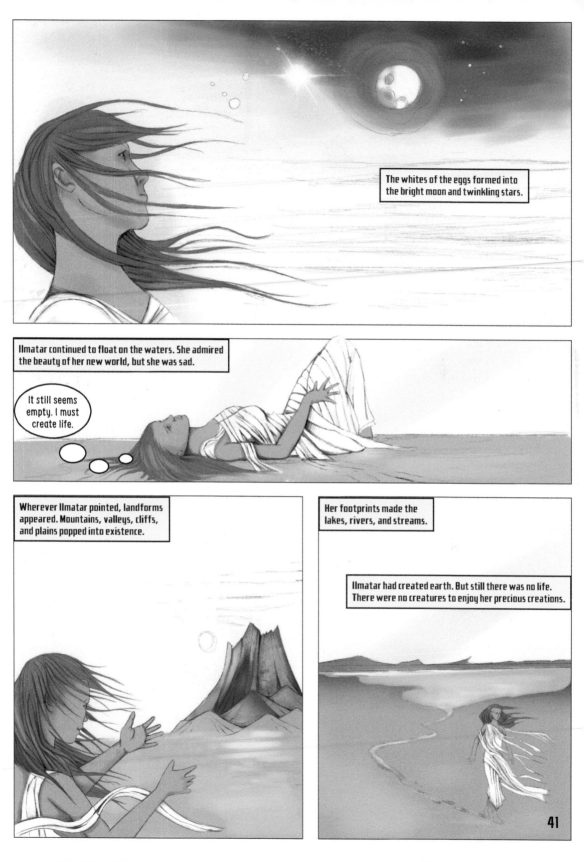

The whites of the eggs formed into the bright moon and twinkling stars.

Ilmatar continued to float on the waters. She admired the beauty of her new world, but she was sad.

It still seems empty. I must create life.

Wherever Ilmatar pointed, landforms appeared. Mountains, valleys, cliffs, and plains popped into existence.

Her footprints made the lakes, rivers, and streams.

Ilmatar had created earth. But still there was no life. There were no creatures to enjoy her precious creations.

One day, Ilmatar gave birth to a son named Vainamoinen [vahy-nuh-MOI-nen]. He was the first human and was born as a wise, old man. The storm winds were his father.

Vainamoinen left Ilmatar and swam in the seas for seven years until he came to an island. He made it his home.

For years I've wandered this empty place. I should bring life and plants to it. But how?

Vainamoinen soon received help with his wish. The gods sent a young boy named Sampsa, who carried seeds. Trees of all kinds sprang up wherever he scattered them.

At last! My island blooms with life.

But one oak tree grew too tall . . .

It hides the sun and brings darkness to the land.

Send help, mother Ilmatar, and return sunlight to the earth!

Ilmatar heard her son's pleas and sent a little man with a copper axe. The man grew into a giant. With three powerful strokes, he cut down the huge oak.

WHAAACK!

He's doing it! Soon the bothersome tree will be no more.

Light was restored and sunshine once again filled the world. The trees grew stronger and taller than ever.

Vainamoinen would later have many adventures and become an important hero in Finnish myths. But we do not know if he ever reunited with his mother, the Goddess of Air, Ilmatar.

DID YOU KNOW?
The Finno-Ugric culture includes about 24 different peoples, including Finns, Hungarians, and Estonians. It is believed that people who speak the various Finno-Ugric languages have lived in Europe for about 10,000 years.

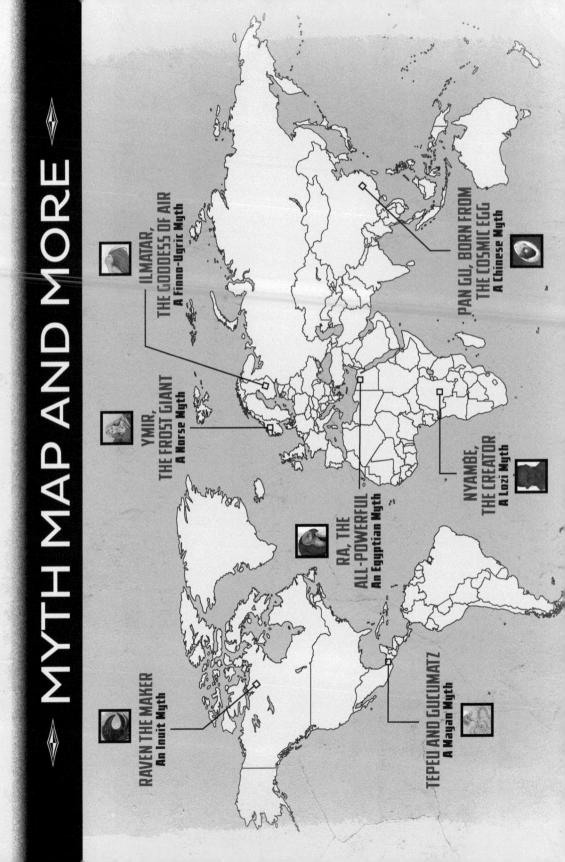

MYTH MAP AND MORE

RAVEN THE MAKER
An Inuit Myth

YMIR,
THE FROST GIANT
A Norse Myth

ILMATAR,
THE GODDESS OF AIR
A Finno-Ugric Myth

PAN GU, BORN FROM
THE COSMIC EGG
A Chinese Myth

RA, THE
ALL-POWERFUL
An Egyptian Myth

NYAMBE,
THE CREATOR
A Lozi Myth

TEPEU AND GUCUMATZ
A Mayan Myth

- The first man and woman that appear in creation myths are often called the "first ancestors." All humanity originates from these two.

- Some creation myths have two or more creators. In Greek mythology, Zeus instructed his two sons to make humans and animals on Earth. In a Japanese myth, one god created all the other gods. In turn, two of the new gods created the islands of Japan.

- Many myths were not written down right away. Instead, people would tell the stories to each other and to their children. The method of passing on stories, beliefs, and histories through speaking instead of writing is called an oral tradition. This is why you can often find slightly different versions of one myth. The story may have changed depending on who was telling it.

- In Norse mythology, dwarves inhabit Nidavellir, a middle world of the Norse universe. The dwarves were created from the vermin that lived in the ice giant Ymir's dead body. Odin, Vili, and Ve gave the vermin intelligence and the bodies of men, but the dwarves decided to live in mountains and caves.

- Creation myths often feature a character called a "culture hero." This individual teaches humans how to survive using technology and new inventions. Pan Gu from the Chinese creation myths is an example of a culture hero.

- The K'iche' Mayan story is an example of an "imperfect creation" myth. Tepeu and Gucumatz realize that mud and wood aren't good materials for making humans, and so they try again. In many creation myths from different cultures, the maker destroys a bad creation by sending a flood.

GLOSSARY

Chaos (KAY-ohs)—in mythology, the dark state in which everything exists but is not yet separate

embers (EM-burz)—the hot, glowing pieces of a fire after the flames are gone

fertility (fuhr-TIL-uh-tee)—the state of being able to produce life; fertility can refer to the ability to grow plants and to the ability to have children

forge (FORJ)—to form by heating and hammering into shape, especially metal

intellect (IN-tuh-lekt)—the power of the mind to think, reason, understand, and learn

pharaoh (FAIR-oh)—the title given to kings in ancient Egypt

quench (KWENCH)—to drink something until no longer thirsty

rampage (RAM-payj)—a violent and excited action

refuge (REF-yooj)—a place that provides shelter and protection

sacred (SAY-krid)—very important and deserving great respect

symbol (SIM-buhl)—a design or an object that stands for something else

READ MORE

Chambers, Catherine. *African Myths and Legends.* All About Myths. Chicago: Heinemann Raintree, 2013.

Hoena, Blake. *Everything Mythology.* National Geographic Kids Everything. Washington, D.C.: National Geographic Books, 2014.

Marsico, Katie. *What We Get From Chinese Mythology.* Mythology and Culture. Ann Arbor, Mich.: Cherry Lake Publishing, 2015.

Yasuda, Anita. *How the World Was Made: A Cherokee Creation Myth.* Minneapolis, Minn.: Magic Wagon, 2013.

CRITICAL THINKING QUESTIONS

1. Being the last person alive on Earth could be a terrible experience in many ways. But what would you do if you were the first being on Earth, like Kamunu, Ymir, or Pan Gu? What would you do? If you had the power to create, what would you make?

2. Now that you've read a few creation myths and understand their basic elements, write your own. Be inventive — you can write a myth about any part of creation. For example, write a myth to explain why volcanoes erupt, or why the sun rises and sets. Create interesting characters and unusual settings to make your myth exciting.

3. Nyambe goes up into the heavens to escape humans. Do you think that was the right decision? What do you think he could have done differently to live in peace with humans? Use evidence from the story to support your answer.

INTERNET SITES

Use FactHound to find Internet sites related to this book.

Visit *www.facthound.com*

Just type in 9781515766292 and go!

INDEX